Brilliant Model Answers

Published by

Educationzone Ltd

London N21 3YA
United Kingdom

C000008859

British Library Cataloguing in Publication Data:

A catalogue record for this publication is available from the British Library.

978-1-906468-90-3

Email us for further information:

info@psychologyzone.co.uk

You can email Nick Savva directly at:

nicksavva@live.co.uk

For more information:

Visit our website for exam questions and answers, teaching resources, books and much more:

www.psychologyzone.co.uk

Content for model answers

Please note: this book is not endorsed by or affiliated to the AQA exam board.

Important information

! *Do not skip this page!*

◾ The 'unpredictable' exam is more 'predictable' than you think

This guide is part of Psychologyzone's Brilliant Model Answers series covering A-level Psychology. Use it alongside the Psychologyzone series Brilliant Exam Notes to get the best out of your learning.

This guide covering the topic of Social Influences provides a full set of exam-style questions and model answers to help you do well in the exam. After all, your psychology exam is based on answering questions – what better than to have a book that already has the answers for you!

The exam board has deliberately developed the A-level Psychology specification so that the questions are to some extent 'unpredictable' in order to discourage students from attempting to rote-learn (memorise answers) using pre-prepared questions. This makes it difficult to predict what's going to be asked.

We have tried to make the unpredictable 'predictable'...

There are over 100 model answers in this book. We have covered most of the different types of question they can ask you for each topic on the specification. You can adapt the model answers provided to most types of questions set in the exam.

◾ Some of your model answers seem very long. Why?

Some of the answers are much longer responses than you are expected to write in the exam to get top marks. This is deliberate. We have written them in this way to enable you to have a better understanding of the theories, concepts, studies and so on. If you do not write as much, don't panic; you don't need all of the content to achieve a good grade.

As you may be using this as a study book, we thought we'd write the model answers in a way that you can also revise from them, so we sometimes expand on explanations or give an example to help you understand a topic better.

Many of the model answers start by repeating the question; in the real exam you do not need to waste time doing this – just get stuck in!

Remember - in your exam, your answers will be marked according to how well you demonstrate the set assessment objectives (AOs); therefore, we have tried to provide model responses that show you how to demonstrate the required know-how for these AOs. Each example provides you with 'indicative content': in other words, the response gives you an idea of points you could make to achieve maximum marks; it doesn't mean these are points you must make. The purpose of these model answers is to inspire you and demonstrate the standard required to achieve top marks.

Exam skills

How will your answer be assessed?

Your teachers will have explained that your answers in the examination will be assessed on what examiners call assessment objectives (AO). If you can familiarise yourself with these AO, this will help you write more effective answers and achieve a higher grade in your exam. There are three assessment objectives called AO1, AO2 and AO3.

By now, your teachers should have given you a lot of practice exam questions and techniques on how to answer them. The aim of this book is not to teach you these skills, but to show you how this is done – to model the answers for you.

Just to remind you, below are the AQA assessment objectives:

 AO1 **Knowledge and understanding**

Demonstrate knowledge and understanding of scientific ideas, processes, techniques and procedures

What does this mean?

The ability to describe psychological theories, concepts, research studies (e.g. aim, procedures, findings and conclusions) and key terms. The exam questions can cover anything that is named on the specification.

Example

Explain the process of synaptic transmission. **[5 marks]**

Outline the role of the somatosensory centre in the brain. **[3 marks]**

 AO2 **Application**

Apply knowledge and understanding of scientific ideas, processes, techniques and procedures:

- in a theoretical context
- in a practical context
- when handling qualitative data
- when handling quantitative data.

What does this mean?

Application questions require you to apply what you have learnt about in Psychology (theories, concepts and studies) to a scenario (situation) often referred to as 'stem' material. A scenario will be a text extract or quote given in the question. You are treated as a psychologist and you need to explain what is going on in the situation from what you have learnt.

Example

Chris suffered a stroke to the left hemisphere of his brain, damaging Broca's area and the motor cortex.

Using your knowledge of the functions of Broca's area and the motor cortex, describe the problems that Chris is likely to experience.   **[4 marks]**

AO2 **Evaluation**

Analyse, interpret and evaluate scientific information, ideas and evidence, including in relation to issues, to:

- make judgements and reach conclusions

- develop and refine practical design and procedures.

What does this mean?

Evaluation simply means assessing the 'value' (hence 'evaluation' of a theory or study you have been describing. There are many ways you can evaluate theories or studies. For students, evaluation often takes the form of the strengths and weaknesses of the theory and/or study, but evaluation can also be in a form of 'commentary' (neither strength nor weakness but more in the form of an 'analysis' – which is still an evaluation).

Example

Outline one strength and one limitation of post-mortem examination.   **[2 marks + 2 marks]**

The different types of exam questions

We have grouped the exam questions into four different types:

Identification questions	Multiple-choice questions, match key words with a definition, tick boxes or place information in some order or in a box.
Short-response questions	Questions worth up to 6 marks (e.g. 1, 2, 3, 4, 5 or 6 marks). These are often questions asking you to 'outline', 'explain', or 'evaluate' a theory or a study.
Application questions	These require you to apply the psychological knowledge you have learnt (theories, concepts and studies) to a real-life scenario given in the exam question.
Long-response question	These deal with long answers worth over 6 marks (8, 12 or 16 marks). The long-response answers found in this book will be mainly for 16-mark questions.

◾ How the model answers are structured

We have tried to structure your learning by breaking down the model answers into four distinct categories

Key terms, concepts, and theories that are named on the AQA specification are covered by the identification and short-response questions (e.g. explain what is meant by the term...).

Research questions asking you to outline a study, describe a theory or give an evaluation are covered by short-response questions (e.g. briefly outline one study that has...).

Application questions require you to apply your knowledge to a made-up scenario (situation) and are covered under application questions.

Essay questions 'Outline and evaluate', or 'Discuss'-type questions are covered under long-response questions. Some long-response questions also require the application of knowledge.

Specification: Memory

- The multi-store model of memory: sensory register, short-term memory and long-term memory. Features of each store: coding, capacity and duration.

- Types of long-term memory: episodic, semantic, procedural.

- The working memory model: central executive, phonological loop, visuo-spatial sketchpad and episodic buffer. Features of the model: coding and capacity.

- Explanations for forgetting: proactive and retroactive interference and retrieval failure due to absence of cues.

- Factors affecting the accuracy of eyewitness testimony: misleading information, including leading questions and post-event discussion; anxiety.

- Improving the accuracy of eyewitness testimony, including the use of the cognitive interview.

The multi-store model of memory

Identification questions

Q1 Below is a diagram of the multi-store model of memory. Review the keywords below, then select the four terms that match A, B, C and D on the diagram and enter the correct letter in the box.

Sensory register

Long-term memory

Central executive

Short-term memory

Rehearsal loop

Phonological store

[4 marks]

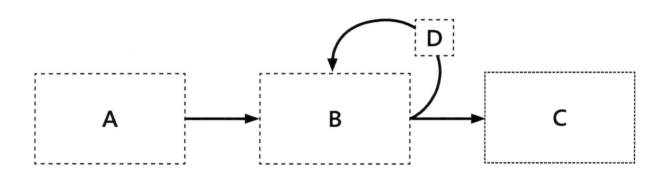

Q2 Complete the missing parts of the table, in relation to features of the multi-store model of memory.

[4 marks]

	Capacity	Duration	Coding
Sensory register		250 milliseconds	Modality specific
Short-term memory	7 +/-2		
Long-term memory	Unlimited	Potentially forever	

Q3 A, B and C relate to memory. Write the appropriate letter in the box below. The first one has been done for you.

    A. 7 ± 2

    B. Up to 30 seconds without rehearsal

    C. Mainly semantically   **[3 marks]**

	Short-term memory	Long-term memory
Encoding		
Capacity	A	
Duration		

Short-response questions

Q4 Explain what is meant by the term 'sensory register'.   **[2 marks]**

The sensory register is a storage system that receives stimuli/information from the environment through the five senses (e.g. eyes, ears, etc.). The sensory register has a very large capacity for storing information but a very limited duration of 250 milliseconds – 2 seconds.

Q5 Explain what is meant by the term 'short-term memory'.   **[2 marks]**

Short-term memory (STM) is a memory storage system that holds information for a short period of time. The duration of information in STM is less than 30 seconds if the information has not been rehearsed. STM also has a limited capacity, approximately 7 plus or minus 2 digits, although this can be increased by chunking (grouping) the digits.

Q6 Explain what is meant by the term 'long-term memory'.   **[2 marks]**

Long-term memory (LTM) is a memory storage system where information is held for a long (or permanent) time. LTM has a potentially unlimited capacity and a duration that can last a lifetime. In terms of coding, long-term memory tends to be coded semantically (the meaning of the experience).

Q7 Explain the difference between short-term and long-term memory. **[3 marks]**

Short-term memory (STM) and long-term memory (LTM) differ in terms of encoding, capacity and duration. In terms of encoding, STM tends to encode information acoustically, whereas information in long-term memory is encoded semantically. The duration of the information held in STM is less than 30 seconds, whereas information held in LTM information may last a lifetime. STM has a limited capacity, approximately 7 plus or minus 2 digits, whereas LTM has a potentially unlimited capacity.

Q8 Explain what is meant by the term 'coding'. **[2 marks]**

Coding is a process of converting information into memory traces so it can be stored and remembered in memory. Information is stored in various forms. For example, short-term memory tends to code information acoustically, whereas information in long-term memory is coded semantically.

Q9 Explain what is meant by the term 'capacity'. **[2 marks]**

Capacity refers to how much information can be held in memory and it is often represented by the number of digits held. Short-term memory has a limited capacity of 7 plus or minus 2 digits (but this can be increased by chunking the digits), while long-term memory has an unlimited capacity.

Q10 Explain what is meant by the term 'duration'. **[2 marks]**

Duration is the amount of time information is held for in memory before it is no longer available. Short-term memory has a very limited duration, less than 30 seconds, if the information is not rehearsed. Long-term memory has a very long duration, possibly a lifetime.

Q11 Describe one study that has investigated coding in memory. **[4 marks]**

Conrad (1964) carried out an experiment to investigate coding in short-term memory. The participants were quickly shown a sequence of six letters that were acoustically similar (such as D, P, T, B, L, V) or acoustically dissimilar (such as K, Z, W, R, Y). The participants had to write down as many letters as they could, in the order they were given to them (to prevent rehearsal). Conrad found that the participants would wrongly recall the order of letters if they were acoustically similar than if they were acoustically dissimilar. This is because the letters sounded like each other, resulting in acoustic confusion and incorrect recall. This study shows that the STM attempts to code information acoustically even when it is presented visually.

Q12 Describe one way in which psychologists have investigated the **duration** of short-term memory. In your answer, you should include details of stimulus materials used, what participants were asked to do and how duration was measured. **[4 marks]**

Peterson and Peterson (1959) carried out an experiment to investigate how long information remains in STM without verbal rehearsal. The participants were briefly presented with a nonsense trigram (e.g. three letters such as CLD, NWQ), immediately followed by a three-digit number (e.g. 882). They were then asked to count backwards in threes from the specified number (e.g. 882, 879, 876) until they were told to stop. This was to prevent them from rehearsing the three to avoid the information remaining fresh in their STM or being transferred to their LTM. To measure the duration of STM, the percentage of trigrams recalled in the correct order was recorded after each time intervals of 3, 6, 9, 12, 15 or 18 seconds.

Q13 Describe one way in which psychologists have investigated the **capacity** of short-term memory. In your answer, you should include details of stimulus materials used, what participants were asked to do and how capacity was measured. **[4 marks]**

Jacob (1887) carried out an experiment to investigate the capacity of the STM by using the serial digit span technique. Participants were presented with a sequence of digits and were required to repeat them back in the same order. They were given one digit to repeat at a time, to begin with, and this gradually increased by one more digit to build up to longer sequences of digits (e.g. 1, 84, 723, 3857, and so on). The capacity of STM was measured by the percentage of correct recall. When the participants failed to recall 50% of the digits, they had reached their digital span capacity.

Q14 Describe one or more studies that have investigated the duration of long-term memory.

[6 marks]

Bahrick et al. (1975) conducted a natural experiment to investigate the duration of LTM, involving nearly 400 American ex-high school students who had left school between 3 months and 48 years ago. The duration was tested by using photographs and names from their high-school yearbook. Bahrick et al. (1975) found participants had 90% correct recall in the photo and name recognition tests even 15 years after graduating high school. Those who left 48 years earlier scored lower (80% for name recognition and 70% for photo recognition). The participants were less accurate in the free recall test (remembering names of ex-classmates), getting 60% correct after 15 years and only 30% after 48 years. The findings provide strong evidence that information is held in LTM for a very long time, although there is some memory loss over time. It also shows that duration of information in LTM is better for visual recognition (photos), than attempting to freely recall information (remembering ex- classmates names without the help of pictures acting as cues).

Q15 Explain why research studies that have investigated the multi-store model (MSM) of memory may be criticised for lacking validity. **[4 marks]**

Research evidence to support the MSM is based on laboratory experiments that may have limited external validity. A laboratory is an artificial setting, so it may lack mundane realism (that is, it does not reflect real life). Some of the memory tasks, such as the use of nonsense trigrams by Peterson and Peterson study to demonstrate the duration of STM, do not reflect how we use our memory in our day-to-day activities in real life. This is because people are not normally asked to remember nonsense trigrams. They may have found this activity meaningless and may not have performed as well as they might have if the experiment was something they could relate to. This is why caution is needed when generalising laboratory findings to the real world.

Application questions

Q16 Josh was asked to remember the following list of numbers: 1, 7, 7, 5, 1, 8, 6, 0, 1, 9, 1, 8, 1, 9, 8, 5. He was able to remember them because he grouped them in this way: 1775, 1860, 1918, 1985. Using what you have learnt about memory, explain why grouping numbers will help Josh remember them. **[4 marks]**

Research evidence has shown that the capacity of short-term memory (STM) can hold between 5 and 9 items. Therefore, Josh would not have been able to remember all the 16 numbers as this would have exceeded the capacity of STM. However, if the items are chunked (grouped) together into smaller segments in a meaningful way, we can increase the amount of information we can store in our STM. This is what Josh has done; he is able to remember the 16 individual numbers because he has chunked them into four smaller segments. However, Simon (1974) found that participants tended to recall fewer chunks when they were large rather than small, which suggests that the amount of information in each chunk size can affect the overall capacity in STM.

Q17 A case study was carried out on Ken, whose brain was damaged in a water sports accident. To test how many numbers he can hold in his short-term memory, psychologists read a list of numbers and asked him to recall the numbers immediately in the correct order. He was only able to recall two numbers. The psychologists found that his long-term memory was normal.

Explain why Ken's short-term memory after the accident is different from most adults' short-term memory. **[2 marks]**

The average capacity of STM for most people is considered to be 7 plus or minus 2 digits. The fact that Ken's was much shorter, in that he could only recall two numbers, suggests that his STM has been damaged in the accident.

Q18 Does Ken's case study (see Q17) support the multi-store model of memory? Explain your answer.

[2 marks]

The above study does support the MSM as this model suggests that memory is made up of separate memory stores, short-memory and long-term and the accident only caused damaged to one store, but not the other store. That is, Ken's short-term memory store was damaged as he could only recall two numbers, but his long-term memory store was OK.

Q19 "The number you require has changed to 02567291923; thank you for calling directory enquiries, please call again soon." Before Mandy could write the number down, she had a short conversation for a few minutes with her mother. Mandy attempted to write the number down on paper, but she had forgotten the number.

Use your knowledge of the multi-store model to explain why Mandy then would not remember the telephone number. **[4 marks]**

Mandy would not remember the number because, according to the MSM, the duration of information in STM fades in less than 30 seconds if it is not rehearsed. The two-minute conversation Mandy had with her mother prevented her from rehearsing the number, so the information faded away during that time they were talking. Also, STM has limited capacity, it can only hold 5-9 items, and the number is longer than that, which meant it had exceeded the capacity; therefore, Mandy could not have remembered it anyway.

Q20 Tom, a psychology student, constantly reads through his revision notes before his examination but finds it difficult to remember the information. However, Tom has no problem remembering the information in a football magazine, even though he has only read it once.

Explain why this can be used as a criticism of the multi-store model of memory. **[4 marks]**

The multi-store model claims that information to be transferred from short-term memory (STM) to long-term memory (LTM) and repeated rehearsal is required in order to be remembered. However, Tom has been reading over and over his revision notes, and yet the information does not transfer from STM to LTM as suggested by the model. Also, the fact that Tom can remember the information in the newspaper from only reading it once shows that rehearsal may not be required to transfer information from STM to LTM.

Q21 A researcher investigating the multi-store model of memory tested short-term memory by reading out loud sequences of numbers that participants then had to repeat aloud immediately after presentation. The first sequence was made up of three numbers: for example, 8, 5, 2. Each participant was tested several times, and each time the length of the sequence was increased by adding another number.

Use your knowledge of the multi-store model of memory to explain the purpose of this research and the likely outcome. **[4 marks]**

The purpose of this experiment is to test the capacity of the STM by using the serial digit span technique. The gradual was increased by one more digit to see how much we can hold in STM. The test was carried out aloud because STM tends to code verbally/acoustically. According to research, most of the people tested would be able to repeat a sequence of between 5 and 9 items correctly.
This is because the multi-store model claims that STM has a limited capacity of 7 + or − 2 digits.

Long-response question

Q22 Describe and evaluate the multi-store model. **[16 marks]**

Atkinson and Shiffrin (1968, 1971) believed there were three components of memory: sensory memory (SM), short-term memory (STM) and long-term memory (LTM). This model attempts to explain how information is processed and flows from one memory store to another store. SM receives and processes information that enters through our senses. SM is modality-specific and has unlimited capacity but limited duration. After 2 seconds, information will fade if it does not receive attention. If the information receives attention, it is transferred into the short-term memory (STM) for processing. The STM has a limited capacity (the magic number 7+/-2) and duration (30 seconds or less) and codes information acoustically. To prevent the information fading in STM, a process of maintenance rehearsal (repetition) is needed. Through rehearsal (mainly verbal or acoustic), information is transferred from STM to LTM. The longer information is rehearsed in STM, the more likely it is to be transferred from STM to LTM for more permanent storage.

Information can be transferred by elaborative rehearsal, where the information is remembered in a meaningful way. LTM has unlimited capacity and unlimited duration, possibly lasting a lifetime, and information is coded semantically. Retrieval is the process of getting information from LTM and involves passing it back through STM, where it is then available for use. However, information can still be lost from LTM, primarily through the processes of interference and retrieval failure.

A strength of the multi-store model is that controlled laboratory studies (e.g. Peterson and Peterson, Baddeley) on capacity, duration and coding support the existence of a separate short and long-term store, which make up the MSM. Furthermore, studies using brain-scanning techniques have also demonstrated a difference between STM and LTM. For example, Beardsley (1997) found that the prefrontal cortex is active during STM but not LTM tasks, and Squire et al. (1992) found the hippocampus is active when LTM is engaged.

The MSM is further supported by research showing STM and LTM are different. For example, Baddeley (1966) found that we tend to mix up words that *sound similar* when using our short-term memory, but we mix up words that have *similar meanings* when we use our long-term memory. This clearly shows that coding in STM is acoustic, and in LTM, it is semantic. This supports the MSM's view that these two memory stores are separate and independent.

However, a criticism of the multi-store model is that it is too simplistic. For example, the MSM oversimplifies LTM by saying it is a single unitary store. However, research evidence shows that LTM is not a unitary store, but there are different storage systems within LTM, and each behaves differently. For instance, there is a storage system for procedural memories (e.g. how to ride a bike), for semantic memories (e.g. knowledge about the world), and for episodic memories (stores events from our lives). This shows that the MSM is limited because it does not reflect these different types of LTM.

A further criticism of the MSM suggests that maintenance rehearsal determines the likelihood that the information will pass into the LTM. However, Craik and Watkins (1973) suggest that elaborative rehearsal (enduring memories), instead of maintenance rehearsal, is more effective in transferring information from the STM into the LTM. This is because enduring memories are processed more deeply and are more memorable.

Furthermore, a study by Tulving's (1967) also showed that maintenance rehearsal is not necessary for transferring information to LTM. This suggests rehearsal in STM may not be necessary to transfer information to LTM storage, but rather that making links with existing knowledge is more effective.

Another criticism is that the research evidence to support the MSM is based on laboratory experiments, which provide an artificial setting that may lack mundane realism (that is, the setting does not reflect real life). Some of the memory tasks used artificial materials, such as the use of nonsense trigrams by the Peterson and Peterson's duration study. These do not reflect how we use our memory in our day-to-day activities in real life because people are not normally asked to remember nonsense trigrams. Participants may have found this activity meaningless and may not have performed as well as they might have if the experiment was something they could relate to. In everyday life, we form memories related to all sorts of useful things – people's faces, names, facts, places, etc. This suggests the MSM lacks external validity. Research findings may reflect how memory works with meaningless material in laboratory testing but do not reflect how memory mainly works in everyday life.

Working memory model

Identification question

Q23 Tick three of the boxes to indicate which of the following are features of the working memory model. **[3 marks]**

- A. Serial position curve ☐
- B. Central executive ☐
- C. Visuo-spatial sketchpad ☐
- D. Phonological loop ☐
- E. Emotional memory store ☐

Short-response questions

Q24 Explain the 'central executive' component of the working memory model. **[4 marks]**

The central executive is in overall charge in STM, and it decides which incoming information from our senses should receive attention and then allocates this information to an appropriate slave system to be processed. The central executive also processes different types of cognitive tasks (e.g. mental arithmetic, reasoning) or retrieving information from LTM. The central executive has a limited duration and capacity.

Q25 Explain the 'phonological loop' component of the working memory model. **[4 marks]**

The phonological loop deals with auditory information. It is divided into the phonological store and the articulatory control process. The phonological loop holds sounds/spoken words for 1-2 seconds. The articulatory process is seen as the 'inner voice' as it allows us to rehearse the sound information held in the phonological store silently to ourselves to prevent it from decaying. The articulatory process also converts written words (e.g. reading a book) into a sound format and then transfers this information to the phonological loop.

Q26 Explain the 'visuo-spatial sketchpad' component of the working memory model. **[4 marks]**

The visuo-spatial sketchpad is known as the 'inner eye' of the STM, as it deals with visual and spatial information (e.g. objects, dimensions). In terms of 'visual' tasks, it can create images from

STM or access them from LTM. It can also process written or sound information and convert this into a mental image. In terms of 'spatial' tasks, it can deal with spatial relations, e.g. the distance or layout of mental images. The visuo-spatial sketchpad can hold a limited amount of visual and spatial information (capacity) and for a limited amount of time (duration).

Q27 Explain the 'episodic buffer' component of the working memory model. **[3 marks]**

The episodic buffer is a temporary store for information. The episodic buffer's role is to interact with the other components (central executive, the phonological loop and visuo-spatial sketchpad) and LTM to combine visual, spatial and sound information to create a single representation (hence 'episode').

An example would be remembering a particular scene from a movie.

Q28 Describe the working memory model. **[6 marks]**

Baddeley and Hitch proposed the working memory model (WMM) to explain how short-term memory (STM) is organised and how it functions. They proposed that STM consists of four systems, each dealing with different types of information. The central executive is in overall charge, and it decides which incoming information should receive attention and then allocates this to an appropriate slave system to be processed. The central executive also processes different cognitive tasks (e.g. mental arithmetic, reasoning), as well as retrieving information from the long-term memory (LTM). The central executive has a limited duration and capacity. The phonological loop deals with auditory information. It is divided into the phonological store, which holds sounds/ spoken words for 1-2 seconds, and the articulatory process. The articulatory process allows us to rehearse the sound information held in the phonological store silently to ourselves to prevent it from decaying. The articulatory process also converts written words (e.g. reading a book) into a sound format and then transfers this information to the phonological loop. The visuo-spatial sketchpad deals with visual and spatial information (e.g. objects, dimensions, layout) in STM or accesses images from LTM. It can also process written or sound information and convert this into a mental image. The visuo-spatial sketchpad can hold a limited amount of visual and spatial information (capacity) and for a limited amount of time (duration). The episodic buffer is a temporary store for information. It interacts with the other components (central executive, phonological loop and visuo-spatial sketchpad) and LTM to combine visual, spatial and sound information to create a single representation, for example, remembering a scene from a movie.

Q29 Describe one or more studies that support the working memory model. **[4 marks]**

Baddeley et al. (1973) provide evidence for the visuo-spatial sketchpad. Participants were asked to follow a visual tracking task while carrying out an imaginary visual task in which they had to describe all the angles found in a capital block letter. The participants found carrying out these tasks very difficult because both required the use of the visuo-spatial sketchpad, resulting in poor performance. However, when the participants performed a list of verbal reasoning tasks and a visual tracking task, they found no difficulty performing both tasks at the same time, because they had to use different slave systems (visual and verbal). This supports the WMM because it shows that the STM has different components for different types of memory tasks.

Application questions

Q30 Monica is applying a memory technique to help her remember information during her GCSE exam. One technique is to visualise an image such as a chair and add the word to be remembered to the image.

Using your knowledge of the working memory model, which component is Monica using?

[1 mark]

Monica is using the visuo-spatial sketchpad component of the working memory model.

Q31 The telephone rings, you pick up the receiver. "Hello. This is Nick", you say into the receiver. "Hi Nick, this is Tom."

Using your knowledge of the working memory model, which component is Tom using?

[1 mark]

Nick is using the phonological loop component of the working memory model.

Q32 Alan was attempting to read the newspaper at the same time as listening to his wife's conversation on the phone with his sister – she is moaning about his lack of help with the housework. Alan finds that he can't really remember much of what he has just read in the newspaper or from his wife's conversation.

Using your knowledge of the working memory model, explain why Alan found it difficult to recall any information.

[4 marks]

According to the working memory model, the reason why Alan could not remember much from his wife's conversation or what he just read from the newspaper is that Alan was using the phonological loop system to deal with both these types of tasks and because the tasks are carried out at the same time, the phonological system is finding it difficult to cope with the demand. Alan is using the phonological store (deals with sound information) to process what his wife is saying, and ar the same time, is using the articulatory control process part of the phonological loop system (converting written information into a sound format) to process what he is reading. The 'overload' of the phonological loop system explains why Alan found it difficult to recall any information.

Q33 A brain scan shows that one area of the brain is more active when a person is doing a verbal task. However, when a person is doing a visual task, a different area is more active.

    a) Explain how this could relate to the working memory model. Refer to different parts of the working memory model in your answer.

[4 marks]

The increase in brain activity in different areas could relate to the working memory model because the model proposes that different components of the working memory will be used to deal with different types of tasks. The phonological loop system of the working memory model deals with sound material. So, any verbal task (e.g. listening to your mum speaking) "will create more activity in a certain area of the brain." The visuo-spatial scratchpad component of the working memory model stores and processes visual and spatial information. So, when any visual task is carried out (e.g. thinking of what your best friend looks like), a different area of the brain will become more active.

> b) Give an example of an appropriate verbal task and an appropriate visual
> task which could be used during the brain scan.   **[1 mark + 1 mark]**

An example of a verbal task could be reading a book.

An example of a visual task could be mentally thinking about what your best friend looks like.

Q34 Ben is drawing his favourite cartoon character from his comic book and listening to his teacher, Mrs Annabel, talk at the same time. Mrs Annabel soon realises what Ben is doing and immediately tells him off. To prove the point that he was not paying attention, she asks him to recall what she has just been saying. Surprisingly, Ben can recall most of what she was just talking about.

Using the working memory model, explain why Ben's memory recall is quite impressive.
                                                                    [4 marks]

Ben's memory recall is impressive because, according to the working memory model, although he is doing two tasks at the same time, Ben's working memory is able to cope with it. This is because the types of tasks (visual and verbal) are different from each other, which means he is using different components of the working memory to deal with them. He is using the visuo-spatial scratchpad component (visual information) to deal with drawing and the phonological loop (sound information) to deal with what Mrs Annabel is saying, so there is no interference. This explains why he can remember what Mrs Annabel said.

Q35 Fiona is at a pub quiz. The next question is a mental arithmetic question: "Work out the answer to 9 times 7, then add this to the answer of 14 times 3. What is the final answer?" Fiona struggles to cope with this question.

Using your knowledge of the working memory model, explain why Fiona has difficulty coping with this arithmetic task.   **[4 marks]**

Fiona is using the phonological loop system (deals with sound) part of the working memory to deal with the tasks. Because she is carrying out more than one task at the same time, the phonological loop is finding it difficult to cope with the demand. She is using the phonological loop to remember the question. She then uses the articulatory control process ("inner voice") of the phonological loop to work out the arithmetic task (9 x 7) and to repeat the number she found to prevent her from forgetting it. At the same, she also needs to work out the other part of the arithmetic task (14 x 3), which may explain why Fiona has difficulty coping with this arithmetic task.

Long-response question

Q36 Describe the working memory model. **[16 marks]**

Baddeley and Hitch proposed the working memory model (WMM) as an explanation of how STM is organised and how it functions. They propose that STM consists of four systems, each dealing with different types of information. The central executive is in overall charge, and it decides which incoming information should receive attention and allocates this to an appropriate slave system to be processed. The central executive also processes different cognitive tasks (e.g. mental arithmetic, reasoning) and retrieving information from LTM. The central executive has a limited duration and capacity. The phonological loop deals with auditory information. It is divided into the phonological store, which holds sounds/spoken words for 1-2 seconds, and the articulatory process. The articulatory process allows us to rehearse the sound information held in the phonological store silently to ourselves to prevent it from decaying. The articulatory process also converts written words (e.g. reading a book) into a sound format and then transfers this information to the phonological loop. The visuo-spatial sketchpad deals with visual and spatial information (e.g. objects, dimensions, layout) in STM or accesses images from LTM. It can also process written or sound information and convert this into a mental image. The visuo-spatial sketchpad can hold a limited amount of visual and spatial information (capacity) and for a limited amount of time (duration). The episodic buffer is a temporary store for information. It interacts with the other components (central executive, phonological loop and visuo-spatial sketchpad) and LTM to combine visual, spatial and sound information to create a single representation. An example would be remembering a particular scene from a movie. There is supporting research evidence for the concept of the visuo-spatial sketchpad. Baddeley et al. (1973) asked participants to follow a visual tracking task while carrying out an imaginary visual task in which they had to describe all the angles found in a capital block letter. The participants found carrying out these tasks very difficult because both required the use of the visuo-spatial sketchpad, resulting in poor performance. However, when the participants performed a list of verbal reasoning tasks and a visual tracking task, they found no difficulty performing both tasks at the same time because they had to use different slave systems (visual and verbal). This supports the WMM because it shows that the STM has different components for different types of memory tasks.

Furthermore, Baddeley et al. (1975) provided evidence for the phonological loop in their word-length effect experiment. They found that, on average, participants can recall lists of words more effectively if the words are short (e.g. sun, belt), rather than long (e.g. aluminium, university). This supports the concept of the articulatory loop because it shows it has a very limited time base capacity, as much as we can rehearse in two seconds. Shorter words take less time to say, so therefore we remember more of them than longer words. The longer words cannot be rehearsed on the phonological loop because they don't fit. However, Baddeley et al.'s (1975) word length effect study has been criticised for low internal validity. It is possible that the participants would have been more familiar with the short words but not so familiar with the longer words, which may explain why participants found it harder to recall longer words and why the shorter words were better recalled. This suggests that the word-length experiment may not be valid in supporting the articulatory loop.

A limitation of the WMM is that there is still little real understanding of the central executive's role and function, which is probably the most crucial part of the model. Exactly what it does and how it works remains speculative. Part of the reason is that there is little experimental support to test the functionalities of the central executive. For example, the central executive is said to have limited capacity, but the actual capacity has not been established. Eysenck (1986) suggested that the central executive might be a single STM store acting independently. Again, the model can only give a partial explanation of STM because it cannot explain adequately how the central executive operates.

There is further support for the WMM from brain-scanning studies. These studies have suggested that different parts of the working memory use different areas of the brain. For example, tasks involving the phonological loop have been located in the Wernicke's area of the brain (dealing with processing speech/sound), and tasks involving the articulatory process have been located in the Broca's area (dealing with speech production). Visuo-spatial sketchpad tasks show that the occipital lobe, which processes visual information, becomes active. Such experimental tasks support the view that there are separate systems, as suggested by the working memory model.

A final weakness of the WMM is that it only explains the processes of the STM and tells us very little about how the working memory system relates to the long-term storage of information. This means the WMM is limited because it only gives us a partial explanation of how memory works.

Types of long-term memory

Identification questions

Q37 Which of the following is more likely to be stored in the episodic long-term memory store?

Circle one letter only. **[1 mark]**

    A. Memories of events that happened at different times on holiday

    B. Factual memories of the different varieties of apples

    C. Being able to understand what a word means

    D. Being able to play the piano

Q38 Complete the following statement about long-term memory.

Circle one letter only. **[1 mark]**

Information stored with reference to time and place refers to:

    A. Episodic memory

    B. Procedural memory

    C. Semantic memory

Q39 Complete the following statement about long-term memory.

Circle one letter only. **[1 mark]**

Information not available for conscious inspection refers to:

    A. Episodic memory

    B. Procedural memory

    C. Semantic memory

Short-response questions

Q40 Using an example, explain what is meant by the 'episodic memory'. **[2 marks]**

Episodic memory is an LTM store for events or experiences that occur in a person's life (life events), for example, remembering what you did on your birthday last year.

Q41 Using an example, explain what is meant by the 'procedural memory'. **[2 marks]**

Procedural memory is an LTM store of how to do things (e.g. motor skills/actions/muscle memories) – for example, driving or riding a bicycle.

Q42 Using an example, explain what is meant by the 'semantic memory'. **[2 marks]**

Semantic memory is an LTM store that contains the knowledge of the world a person has learnt, e.g. facts, concepts, meanings, and the functions of objects – for example, knowing the name and function of a screwdriver.

Q43 Explain two differences between procedural memory and episodic memory. **[4 marks]**

Procedural memory is non-declarative memory, which means that it does not require conscious thought or effort, whereas episodic (and semantic) memory is seen as a declarative memory, which means it requires conscious thought or effort.

Procedural memory is the LTM store of how to do things (e.g. motor skills/actions/muscle memories); whereas with episodic memories, LTM stores contain events or experiences that occur in a person's life.

Q44 Explain two differences between semantic and episodic memory. **[4 marks]**

Semantic memories are general knowledge about the world (e.g. facts, concepts, meanings, and the functions of objects), whereas procedural memories are an LTM store of how to do things (e.g. motor skills/actions/muscle memories).

Semantic memories can often recall when and where we learned information, but with episodic memories, we are unable to recall when and where we learnt how to do things.

Q45 Explain what is meant by the 'episodic memory'.　　　　　　　　　**[6 marks]**

Episodic memory is memories that are held in the LTM store for events or experiences that occur in a person's life, for example, remembering what you did on your birthday last year. You may recall the time and place, as well as who was there. Episodic memories are 'time-stamped' – in other words, you remember the 'time' this specific event happened. Episodic memory is seen as a declarative memory, which means it requires conscious thought or effort to recall such memories. The prefrontal cortex is associated with the initial coding of episodic memories. However, memories of the different parts of the event are located in the different visual and auditory parts of the brain but are connected together in the hippocampus (where episodic memories are formed) to create a memory of an episode.

Q46 Explain what is meant by the 'procedural memory'.　　　　　　　　　**[6 marks]**

Procedural memory is memories that are held in the LTM store of how to do things (e.g. motor skills/actions/muscle memories) – for example, driving, or riding a bicycle, or knowing how to write. Procedural memory is non-declarative memory, which means it does not require conscious thought or effort to recall these things as they occur automatically. This allows people to simultaneously perform other cognitive tasks at the same time, e.g. driving and changing gear without even recalling how and talking to a friend at the same time. Procedural memories are encoded and stored by the cerebellum, prefrontal cortex and motor cortex and are all engaged early in learning motor skills. Procedural memories do not appear to involve the hippocampus at all to function.

Q47 Explain what is meant by the 'semantic memory'.　　　　　　　　　**[6 marks]**

Semantic memory is memories that are held in the LTM store that contain knowledge of the world a person has learnt. These memories are also shared by everyone, e.g. facts, concepts, meanings, and the functions of objects, for example, knowing the name and function of a screwdriver. Semantic memories are not 'time-stamped' – in other words, we do not remember where we first learnt them. For example, we do not remember when we learnt about the singer Selena Gomez. There is disagreement about which part of the brain is involved in semantic LTM. Some evidence suggests it is the prefrontal cortex, the hippocampus and the related areas, while others believe that semantic knowledge is widely distributed across all brain areas.

Application question

Q48 Annie can still skateboard even though she hasn't skated for many years.

Germaine can still recall what happened on his first day at university, even though it was ages ago. Billy remembers the names of the tools he needs to repair the broken tap.

Identify three types of long-term memory and explain how each type is shown in one of the examples above. **[6 marks]**

In Annie's case, her remembering how to skateboard is an example of procedural memory. This is because she remembers an action or muscle-based memory.

In Germaine's case, what she remembers is an example of episodic memory. This is because she recalls the events that took place at a specific point in time.

In Billy's case, his remembering the names of tools is an example of semantic memory. This is because he remembers factual information about tools and their use.

Long-response question

Q49 Describe and evaluate types of long-term memory. **[16 marks]**

Episodic memories are memories held in the long-term memory (LTM) store for events or experiences that occur in a person's life (life events). For example, remembering what you did on your birthday last year. Episodic memories are 'time-stamped' – in other words, you remember the 'time' this specific event happened, as well as other several elements – people, places, objects, and behaviours, are woven into one memory. You may also recall associated emotions that you felt at the time.

Procedural memories are long-term memories held in the LTM store of how to do things (e.g. motor skills/actions/muscle memories) – for example, driving and riding a bicycle. Procedural memory is non-declarative memory, which means it does not require conscious thought or effort to recall these things as they occur automatically. This allows people to simultaneously perform other cognitive tasks at the same time, e.g. driving and changing gear without even recalling how and talking to a friend at the same time.

Semantic memories are memories that are held in the LTM store that contain the knowledge of the world a person has learnt, which is also shared by everyone, e.g. facts, concepts, meanings, and the functions of objects – for example, knowing the name and function of a screwdriver. Semantic memories are not 'time-stamped' – in other words, we do not remember where we first learnt them. For example, we do not remember when we learnt about the singer Selena Gomez.

There is research evidence to support the different types of long-term memory. There is the case study about Clive Wearing, who suffered brain damage from a virus that made his brain swell. This left Clive with virtually no episodic memory, for example, he could not recall the names of his children. His procedural and semantic memory stores were still fully intact (he could still play the piano). This case study suggests that there are different memory stores in the LTM. One store can be damaged (in this case, Clive's semantic memory), but leave the other stores unaffected (procedural and semantic).

Further strength for the explanations into the different types of long-term memory are that it is supported by neuroimaging studies (images of brain activity). For example, in a study by Tulving et al. (1994), the participants performed various memory tasks while their brain activity was scanned using a positron emission tomography (PET) scanner. They found that the episodic and semantic memories were both recalled from an area of the brain known as the prefrontal cortex. This area is divided into two, one corresponding to each side (hemisphere) of the brain. The left prefrontal cortex was involved in recalled semantic memories, and the right was involved in recalled episodic memories. This study is a strength because it supports the view that there is a physical reality to the different types of LTM within the brain.

However, a weakness of the research that supports the different types of LTM is that it has low population validity. This is because a large body of supporting evidence is based on case studies of patients with brain damage. This is a criticism because the sample used in this research, such as Clive Wearing, may not be representative of the wider population. For example, just because Clive Wearing's memory was selectively damaged doesn't mean that other people who suffer brain damage in the same areas of the brain would present with the same memory problems. Before his illness, Clive Wearing was a highly intelligent, articulate and professional male in his early 40's. Therefore, we cannot generalise the findings of this case study to the wider population.

A further criticism is that episodic and semantic memories are different memory types, and these memories may not be totally correct. Although research evidence suggests different brain areas for semantic and episodic memories, there is a lot of overlap between the two memory systems. This is because many semantic memories originate as episodic memory. This is an issue because we cannot be sure that a transformation of an episodic memory into semantic means a change is happening in a different type of memory system. Cohen and Squire (1980) argued that episodic and semantic memories are stored together in one LTM store called declarative memory (memories that can be consciously recalled). Cohen and Squire agree that procedural memory is a distinctly different kind of memory to semantic/episodic and call it non-declarative memory. It is important to understand the distinction between semantic and episodic memories because the way we define them influences how memory studies are researched.

Explanations for forgetting: Interference

Identification questions

Q50 Proactive interference is an explanation for forgetting. Which memory store does proactive interference occur in?

Circle one letter only. **[1 mark]**

    A. Short-term memory

    B. Long-term memory

    C. Sensory memory

    D. Echoic memory

Q51 Retroactive interference is an explanation for forgetting. Identify which statements are examples of retroactive interference.

Circle two letters only. **[2 marks]**

    A. Adam revises for his Spanish exam, then for his French exam, and has trouble recalling his Spanish.

    B. Adam revises for his French exam, then for his Spanish exam, and has trouble recalling his Spanish.

    C. Adam has a new mobile phone number, but he keeps accidentally telling people the old one.

    D. Adam accidentally calls his new girlfriend by his old girlfriend's name.

Short-response questions

Q52 Explain what is meant by 'retroactive interference' as an explanation for forgetting. **[3 marks]**

Retroactive interference is when new information interferes with previous information, causing us to forget or poorly recall the information previously learned. For example, a teacher learns the names of this year's psychology class but cannot remember the names of his previous students.

Q53 Explain what is meant by 'proactive interference' as an explanation for forgetting. **[3 marks]**

Proactive interference is when past information interferes with new information, causing us to forget or poorly recall the new information. For example, if you change your telephone number, every time you attempt to recall the new number, the old number will disrupt attempts to recall the new number.

Q54 Describe 'interference' as an explanation for forgetting. **[6 marks]**

Interference theory is an explanation for forgetting in long-term memory. Interference theory suggests that forgetting occurs because two sets of information that are relatively similar become confused (interfere) with each other, resulting in forgetting or distorting of one or both. The more similar the information, the more likely interference will occur. Retroactive interference is when new information interferes with previous information, causing us to forget or poorly recall the information previously learned. For example, a teacher learns the names of this year's psychology class but cannot remember the names of his previous students. Proactive interference is when past information interferes with new information, causing us to forget or poorly recall the new information. For example, if you change your telephone number, every time you attempt to recall the new number, the old number will disrupt attempts to recall the new number.

Q55 Describe one study of 'interference' as an explanation for forgetting. **[4 marks]**

McGeogh and McDonald (1931) gave participants lists of words to learn until they could recall them with 100% accuracy. After 10 minutes, they were then given a new list to learn. The new material varied in the degree to which it was similar to the old original words, depending on the group.

Group 1 – words had the same meanings as the originals.

Group 2 – words had opposite meanings to the originals.

Group 3 – words unrelated to the original ones.

Group 4 – nonsense syllables.

Group 5 – three-digit numbers.

Group 6 – no new list.

They found that the recall performance of the original words depended on the nature of the second list. The most similar material (synonyms) produced the worst recall. When the participants were given very different material, such as three-digit numbers, the mean number of items recalled increased. This shows that retroactive interference affected recall, as it indicates that the more similar the later word, the greater level of forgetting.

Long-response question

Describe and evaluate 'interference' as an explanation for forgetting. **[16 marks]**

Interference theory is an explanation for forgetting in long-term memory. Interference theory suggests that forgetting occurs because two sets of information that are relatively similar become confused (interfere) with each other, resulting in forgetting or distortion of one or both. The more similar the information, the more it is that likely interference will occur. Retroactive interference is when new information interferes with previous information, causing us to forget or poorly recall the information previously learned. For example, a teacher learns the names of this year's psychology class but cannot remember the names of his previous students. Proactive interference is when past information interferes with new information, causing us to forget or poorly recall the new information. For example, if you change your telephone number, every time you attempt to recall the new number, the old number will disrupt attempts to recall the new number.

There is experimental research evidence to support proactive interference explanation for forgetting. Keppel and Underwood (1962) carried out an experiment similar to the Peterson and Peterson (1959) duration study. They found that when participants were presented with a list of meaningless three-letter consonant trigrams (e.g. XVW) they had previously learned, the more likely they were to forget the new task (recalling a nonsense syllable) after 24 hours delay. This demonstrates that proactive interference occurred: a memory of the earlier consonants, which had transferred to long-term memory, was interfering with the memory for new consonants due to the similarity of the information presented.

There is experimental research evidence to support retroactive interference explanation for forgetting. McGeogh and McDonald (1931) gave participants lists of words to learn until they could recall them with 100% accuracy. After 10 minutes, participants were then given a new list to learn. The new material varied in the degree to which it was similar to the old original words. McGeogh and McDonald found that the recall performance for the original words depended on the nature of the second list. The most similar material (synonyms) produced the worst recall. When the participants were given very different material to recall, such as three-digit numbers, the mean number of items recalled increased. This shows that retroactive interference affected recall, as it indicates that the more similar the later material, the greater the level of forgetting.

However, there is opposing research evidence for the interference theory. Tulving and Psotka (1971) gave participants five lists. Each list contained 24 words to remember and was organised into categories (e.g. fruits, animals, etc.). Recall was about 70% for the first list, but this fell as each additional list was learned, presumably due to interference. However, when given a cued recall test (the participants were told the names of the categories), recall rose again to about 70%. This shows that the memories of the words were stored in the LTM, but interference prevented access to them. When given a cue, participants found it easier to access the forgotten words.

Furthermore, many studies used to support interference theory are laboratory-based and therefore represent a more artificial test of memory, which does not reflect everyday memory. For example, many of the materials used are lists of words, with a task attached to learn them. This differs from things we try to learn every day, e.g. people's faces, birthdays, details of psychological research, etc.

This is an issue because these materials are artificial compared to everyday life, meaning that it is difficult to generalise these findings to real life. As a result, the ecological validity of these pieces of research is questioned, which in turn casts doubt over the validity of interference as an explanation for forgetting in everyday life.

Finally, another criticism of interference theory is that it only explains forgetting when two sets of information are similar, for example, when simultaneously learning two languages, such as French and Spanish. This does not happen very often, and so interference cannot explain forgetting in the majority of real-life situations when information is not similar.

Explanations for forgetting: Retrieval failure

Identification question

Q57 Retrieval failure is an explanation for forgetting. Identify the statement that correctly explains why retrieval failure occurs.

Circle one letter only. **[1 mark]**

    A. Information has decayed from memory and is no longer available.

    B. The cues at the time of memory recall are missing.

    C. Information was not encoded corrected correctly at the time of learning.

    D. There are too many cues, and we get confused.

Short-response questions

Q58 Explain what is meant by 'absence of cues' as an explanation for forgetting. **[2 marks]**

Cues are clues or prompts that trigger our memory to remember things. Cues can be environmental things, e.g. location, or linked to our mental state (being sad). Retrieval of information depends on using these cues. If these cues are not present at the time of recall, then retrieval failure happens, and you cannot recall the information effectively.

Q59 Explain what is meant by 'retrieval failure' as an explanation for forgetting. **[3 marks]**

Retrieval failure is the failure to recall information because we have insufficient cues (clues) to trigger our memory. The context where initial learning takes place or our mood at the time may act as a cue later when we are trying to recall. The absence of these cues will lead to greater forgetting.

Q60 Describe 'retrieval failure' as an explanation for forgetting. **[6 marks]**

Retrieval failure theory is an explanation for forgetting in long-term memory (LTM). According to this theory, forgetting happens because of the absence/insufficiency of appropriate cues (triggers/clues) to trigger our memory. Tulving and Thomson (1973) proposed that memory recall is most effective if cues that were present at encoding (learning) are also available at the time of retrieval. If these cues are not available at the time of recall, forgetting is more likely to occur. According to the encoding specificity principle, the cue doesn't have to be exactly the same, but the closer the cue is to the original item, the more likely we will remember the information. There is evidence that cues that have been explicitly or implicitly encoded at the time of learning often have a meaningful connection to the learning material. For example, the cue 'magic 7+/- 2' may lead you to recall all sorts of information about the capacity of short-term memory.

There is another type of cue that is not related to the learning material in any meaningful way. Context-dependent failure states that forgetting is more likely to occur when external/environment cues, e.g. the location, weather, or people, are different at recall from the time of learning. One example would be getting a lower score in a test when sitting in an unfamiliar room than when sitting the test in your normal room. State-dependent failure suggests that forgetting is more likely to occur when internal cues, that is, the individual's internal state of mind (e.g. feeling upset, happy, drunk, etc.) is dissimilar at recall to when the information was initially encoded, which will limit the amount of information we are able to recall.

Q61 Describe one study of 'retrieval failure' as an explanation for forgetting. **[4 marks]**

Godden & Baddeley (1975) asked underwater divers to learn and recall a list of words. The conditions were:

Group 1: Learn on land – recall on land.

Group 2: Learn on land – recall underwater.

Group 3: Learn underwater – recall on land.

Group 4: Learn underwater – recall underwater.

They found that accurate recall was 40% lower in the non-matching environmental context conditions (e.g. learn underwater – recall on land) than when the environment did match (i.e. conditions 1 and 4). This study showed that context-dependent forgetting occurred because the information was not accessible – they forgot when context at recall did not match context at learning.

Application questions

Q62 Toby and Sarah both studied AS Psychology at the same school. Toby's class was taught in the school's lecture theatre, while Sarah's class had their lessons in a science classroom. Both students sat their final psychology exam in the school's lecture theatre.

Which student is likely to perform worse in their final psychology exam? Use your knowledge of explanations of forgetting to justify your answer. **[4 marks]**

Sarah is likely to perform worse. This is according to the encoding specificity principle, which states that if the cues at the time of learning are absent at the time of recall, we are more likely to forget.

Therefore, the cues present when learning the psychology material in the classroom would not have been present at recall in the lecture theatre for Sarah. This means that Sarah did not have any triggers to aid her recall, and this caused retrieval failure.

Long-response questions

Q63 Describe and evaluate 'retrieval failure' as an explanation for forgetting. **[16 marks]**

Retrieval failure theory is an explanation for forgetting in long-term memory (LTM). According to this theory, forgetting happens because of the absence/insufficiency of appropriate cues (triggers/ clues) to trigger our memory. Tulving and Thomson (1973) proposed that memory recall is the most effective when cues that were present at encoding (learning) are also available at the time of retrieval. If these cues are not available at the time of recall, forgetting is more likely to occur. According to the encoding specificity principle, the cue doesn't have to be exactly the same, but the closer the cue is to the original item, the more likely we will remember the information. There is evidence that cues that have been explicitly or implicitly encoded at the time of learning often have a meaningful connection to the learning material. For example, the cue 'magic 7+/- 2' may lead you to recall all sorts of information about the capacity of short-term memory.

There is another type of cue that is not related to the learning material in any meaningful way. Context-dependent failure states that forgetting is more likely to occur when external/environment cues, e.g. the location, weather, people, are different at recall from the time of learning. One example is getting a lower score in a test when sitting in an unfamiliar room than when sitting the test in your normal room. State-dependent failure suggests that forgetting is more likely to occur when internal cues (the individual's internal state of mind, e.g. feeling upset, happy, drunk, etc.) are dissimilar at recall to when the information was initially encoded, which will limit the amount of information we are able to recall.

A strength of retrieval failure theory is that it has supporting experimental research evidence. Godden & Baddeley (1975) asked underwater divers to learn word lists either on dry land or underwater. They then had to recall the words in the same setting (e.g. learning on land and recalling on land) or the opposite setting (e.g. learning on land and recalling underwater). They found that accurate recall was 40% lower in the non-matching environmental context conditions (e.g. learn underwater – recall on land) than when the environment did match. This study showed that context-dependent forgetting occurred because the information was not accessible – they forgot when context at recall did not match context at learning.

However, there is contradictory evidence that questions the retrieval failure theory as an effective explanation for forgetting. Baddeley (1997) argues that the actual ability of the 'context' to influence recall may not be very strong. Baddeley argues that the different contexts have to be very different before they can have an impact on memory (e.g. land vs underwater as a very extreme example).

Learning something in one room then recalling it in another is unlikely to result in much forgetting because these environments are not sufficiently different. As a consequence, the overall credibility of the theory of retrieval failure theory is weakened.

A further weakness of retrieval failure theory is that most of the research carried out has been held in laboratory experiments. Such situations represent a more artificial test of memory that is not similar to a real-life experience. Furthermore, some memories are not dependent on cues. Procedural memories (knowing how to do things) are not related to cue dependent recall. For example, skills such as riding a bike or playing tennis are not forgotten and not affected by retrieval cues. As a result, cue-dependent recall may not apply to some aspects of how we use memory in everyday life.

However, there is real-life anecdotal evidence to support the view that the retrieval failure theory has relevance to everyday memory experience. People often report context-related cues experiences. For example, a person may go downstairs to get an item and then forget what they came downstairs for. However, when they go back upstairs, they remember again. The application is that when we have trouble remembering something, it is probably worth trying to revisit the environment in which we first experienced it. This is a basic principle of the cognitive interview, a method of getting eyewitnesses to recall more information about crimes by using a technique called 'context reinstatement'.

Eyewitness testimony (EWT): misleading information

Identification question

Q64 Identify which of the following is a misleading question. **[1 mark]**

Circle one letter only.

A. Question A "How old was the youth in the shop?"

B. Question B "How old was the man in the shop?"

Short-response questions

Q65 Explain what is meant by the term 'eyewitness testimony'. **[2 marks]**

Eyewitness testimony (EWT) is when a person witnesses an act such as a crime or an accident and is asked to recall what they saw from memory. The accuracy of EWT can be affected by factors such as misleading information, leading questions, and anxiety.

Q66 Explain what is meant by the term 'leading question' in the context of EWT. **[2 marks]**

The term 'leading question' refers to a question given to the eyewitness, usually after the event, that has been phrased in a particular way that leads them to the desired answer.

Q67 Explain what is meant by the term 'misleading question' in the context of EWT. **[2 marks]**

The term 'misleading question' refers to the information given to the eyewitness, usually after the event, which may lead a witness's memory of the incident to be changed. It can take many forms, such as leading questions or post-event discussion between co-witnesses and/or other people.

Q68 Explain what is meant by the term 'post-event discussion' in the context of EWT. **[2 marks]**

Post-event discussion is a type of misleading information whereby conversation between the interviewer or co-witnesses and the eyewitness after the crime has taken place may contaminate the eyewitness's memory of the event through having the discussion.

Q69 Explain how 'post-event discussion' might lead to inaccuracy in eyewitness testimony.

[3 marks]

Post-event discussion is a type of misleading information whereby the conversation between the interviewer or co-witnesses and the eyewitness after the crime has taken place may contaminate the witness's memory of the event through having the discussion. This might create inaccurate recall in eyewitness testimony.

Q70 Identify and outline two factors that may affect the accuracy of eyewitness testimony.

[4 marks]

One factor that may affect the accuracy of eyewitness testimony is the use of leading questions. These are questions given to the eyewitness, usually after the event, that have been phrased in a particular way that leads the eyewitness to the desired answer.

Another factor that may affect the accuracy of eyewitness testimony is post-event discussion. This refers to a conversation between the interviewer or co-witnesses and the eyewitness after the crime has taken place, which may contaminate the witness's memory of the event through having the discussion.

Q71 Describe at least one research study that has investigated the effects of misleading information on eyewitness testimony. In your answer, you should include details of what participants were asked to do and what results were found.

[4 marks]

Loftus and Palmer (1974) carried out an experiment to see whether giving participants leading questions would affect the accuracy of their memory recall. They asked 45 participants to watch slides of a car accident. The participants were put into groups, each of nine participants.

They were then given a questionnaire to answer about the incident. The independent variable was the verb that described how the cars contacted each other, and the dependent variable was the 'speed estimation' the students reported. One group was given the leading question, 'About how fast were the cars going when they "smashed" into each other?' (The leading word 'smashed' suggests the car was travelling quite fast.) The other groups were given the same question but with another verb, such as "hit", "collided", "bumped" and "contacted" (all of which suggest a slower speed), instead of the word "smashed". Loftus and Palmer found that participants who were asked how fast the cars were going when they "smashed" into each other estimated the speed to be, on average, 40.8 mph, while those who were asked how fast the cars were going when they "contacted" each other gave an average speed estimate of 31.8 mph. This shows that leading questions affect the response of eyewitnesses.

Q72 Describe at least one research study that has investigated post-event discussion as a factor affecting the accuracy of eyewitness testimony. In your answer, you should include details of what participants were asked to do and what results were found. **[4 marks]**

Gabbert et al. (2003) investigated the effect of post-event discussion on the accuracy of eyewitness testimony. The researchers got paired participants to watch a video of the same crime, a girl stealing money from a wallet, but the event had been filmed in a way that each participant could see elements that the other could not. After the video, both participants discussed what they had seen before individually completing a test of recall. Gabbert et al. found that a very high number of participants (71%) mistakenly recalled aspects of the event that they did not see in the video but had picked up during the post-event discussion. In a control group, where there was no discussion, there were no errors. This shows that post-event discussion can affect the response of eyewitnesses.

Q73 Explain why studies of eyewitness testimony have been criticised for lacking validity. **[5 marks]**

Many of the studies have investigated EWT by conducting laboratory experiments such as the Loftus experiment into eyewitness testimony and the effect of leading questions on memory recall. This approach has been criticised because under such laboratory conditions, with the procedures used, the findings into EWT may be low in ecological validity because they lack mundane realism (they do not reflect real life). For example, witnessing a video of a crash in a laboratory is different from experiencing one in real life. It could be argued that the participants are aware that something interesting is going to be shown to them, and thus their attention level will be higher than normal. In real life, eyewitnesses are often taken by surprise and often fail to pay close attention to the event or incident. This means caution is needed when generalising findings from artificial experimental settings to real life as the situations are completely different.

Long-response question

Q74 Describe and evaluate misleading information as a factor affecting the accuracy of eyewitness testimony. **16 marks]**

Loftus and Palmer (1974) investigated the effects of leading questions on the accuracy of eyewitness testimony. They asked 45 participants to watch slides of a car accident. The participants were put into groups and were then given a questionnaire to answer about the incident. One group was given the leading question, 'About how fast were the cars going when they "smashed" into each other?' The other four groups were given the same question but with another verb: "hit", "collided", "bumped" and "contacted" instead of the word "smashed". Loftus and Palmer found that participants who were asked how fast the cars were going when they "smashed" into each other estimated the speed to be, on average, 40.8 mph, while those who were asked how fast the cars were going when they "contacted" each other gave an average speed estimate of 31.8 mph. This shows that leading questions affect the response of eyewitnesses.

Gabbert et al. (2003) investigated the effect of post-event discussion on the accuracy of eyewitness testimony. The researchers got paired participants to watch a video of the same crime, a girl stealing money from a wallet, but the video had been filmed in a way that each participant could see elements that the other could not. After watching the video, both participants discussed what they had seen before individually completing a test of recall. Gabbert et al. found that a very high number of participants (71%) mistakenly recalled aspects of the event that they did not see in the video but had picked up during the post-event discussion. In a control group, where there was no discussion, there were no errors. This shows that post-event discussion can affect the response of eyewitnesses.

The strength of research evidence into misleading information is that the studies take place in a highly controlled setting. This meant that the experimenter could control or eliminate any potential extraneous (unwanted) variables such as demand characteristics, the time allowed to answer and individual differences among the students (e.g. in their age and gender). This ensured that the unwanted variables would not affect the respondents' answers, which meant that the researchers were confident in establishing a causal relationship between the independent variables (IV) (misleading question) and the dependent variables (DV - accuracy of memory recall in terms of the speed of the cars). This means the study can be easily repeated by other researchers, using the same experimental conditions and procedures to see whether they get similar results. Other researchers have shown similar results, which means that these studies are reliable and valid.

A further strength is that research into misleading information has real-life usage. The research has led to important practical uses for police officers and investigators because the consequences of inaccurate EWT can be very serious. Loftus (1975) claimed that leading questions could have such a distorting influence on memory that police officers need to be careful about how they phrase questions when interviewing eyewitnesses. Research into EWT is one area where psychologists can make an important difference to the lives of real people, e.g. by improving how the legal system works and acting as expert witnesses.

However, others have criticised experimental research into EWT, as it may be low in ecological validity because it lacks mundane realism (real life). Witnessing a video of a crash in a laboratory is different from experiencing one in real life. It could be argued that the participants were aware that something interesting was going to be shown to them, and thus their attention level would have been higher than normal. In real life, eyewitnesses are often taken by surprise and often fail to pay close attention to the event or incident. As a result, we cannot be sure that misleading information does, in fact, impact eyewitness testimony in real life as we cannot generalise the results outside the lab setting. As a result, this reduces the overall validity of the research evidence.

Furthermore, Loftus' laboratory studies were based on a narrow sample type. University students differ from the general population in terms of their age and education level. Also, students are in an environment where they are continually memorising information, so they are probably good at remembering things. This means that the research findings cannot be generalised to the wider population. However, the study by Gabbert et al. tested two different populations - university students and older adults - and found little difference between these two conditions. Therefore, her results provide good population validity and allow us to conclude that post-event discussion affects younger and older adults in a similar way.

Eyewitness testimony (EWT): anxiety

Short-response questions

Q75   Explain how anxiety might affect the accuracy of eyewitness testimony.   **[3 marks]**

Anxiety may have a negative effect on the accuracy of eyewitness testimony. This is because we are so anxious that we focus on how we are feeling and not on the event itself. Research has shown that stress has a negative effect on our memory, so we recall less about the event than we would if we had not been feeling anxious at the time.

Q76   Describe one study into anxiety as a factor affecting the accuracy of eyewitness testimony. Include in your answer what the researcher(s) did and what they found.   **[6 marks]**

Johnson and Scott (1976) carried out a laboratory experiment to investigate the effect of a weapon on memory recall. They asked participants to sit in a waiting room where they heard an argument taking place in the next room. They then witnessed a man run through the room carrying either a pen covered in grease (low anxiety) or holding a paper knife with his hands covered in blood (high anxiety 'weapon focus'). The participants were later asked to identify the man from a set of 50 photographs. The researchers found that the man carrying the pen was identified 49% of the time, whilst the man carrying the knife was recognised only 33% of the time. The study shows that anxiety arising from the presence of a weapon distracts attention from other details and therefore reduces the accuracy of witness recall.

Application questions

Q77   Elsie was at a jewellery shop, where Lillie was choosing her engagement ring, when a man burst into the shop armed with a shotgun and threatened a member of staff before fleeing with thousands of pounds' worth of gold and silver jewellery. Elsie was so terrified of the ordeal that she had difficulty recalling the events to the police.

Explain why anxiety might have affected Elsie to recall the events. Refer to psychological research in your answer.   **[4 marks]**

Johnson and Scott (1976) found that participants who were exposed to a scene of a man holding a weapon (e.g. knife) were less able to identify (33%) the man from a set of 50 photographs sometime later, compared to those participants in the 'no weapon' scene (49%). The study shows that anxiety arising from the presence of a weapon distracts attention from other details and therefore reduces the accuracy of witness recall. Therefore, this suggests that Elsie's focus on the weapon may have reduced the accuracy of recall. The presence of a dangerous weapon (e.g. gun)

heightens anxiety levels, which then increases attention to 'focus in' on the weapon, drawing our attention away from other details of the crime (e.g. facial features, clothing, details of the crime scene), which explains why recall of events is sometimes poor.

Long-response question

 Q78   Describe and evaluate anxiety as a factor affecting the accuracy of eyewitness testimony.

[16 marks]

Anxiety may have negative and positive effects on recall. Johnson and Scott (1976) carried out a laboratory experiment to investigate the effect of a weapon on memory recall. They asked participants to sit in a waiting room where they heard an argument taking place in the next room. They then witnessed a man run through the room carrying either a pen covered in grease (low anxiety) or holding a paper knife with his hands covered in blood (high anxiety 'weapon focus'). The participants were later asked to identify the man from a set of 50 photographs. The researchers found that the man carrying the pen was identified 49% of the time, whilst the man carrying the knife was recognised only 33% of the time. The study shows that anxiety arising from the presence of a weapon distracts attention from other details and therefore reduces the accuracy of witness recall.

In contrast, Yuille and Cutshall (1986) found a very accurate recall of a real-life shooting up to five months after the event. Participants who reported the highest levels of stress (questionnaire) were most accurate (about 88% compared to 75% for the less stressed group) in recalling events that matched their initial detailed report to the police. This suggests that anxiety can enhance the accuracy of EWT. One possible explanation for why there has been contradictory evidence was provided by Yerkes and Dodson (1980). They proposed that an inverted 'U' relationship exists between stress and the accuracy of memory recall. This relationship suggests that accuracy of recall is at its highest when there is a moderate level of anxiety (optimal point), and then the accuracy of recall declines if the anxiety levels increase above or decrease below the optimal point.

One limitation of the research is that weapon focus may not be caused by anxiety. Pickel (1998) argues that Johnson and Scott's research may be testing 'surprise' rather than anxiety. To test this, she conducted an experiment for participants to watch a thief enter a hairdressing salon carrying, in turn, scissors (high threat, low surprise), a handgun (high threat, high surprise), a wallet (low threat, low surprise) or a raw chicken (low threat, high surprise). She found that identification was least accurate in the high-surprise conditions rather than the high threat. This suggests that the weapon-focus effect is due to unusualness (surprise) rather than anxiety. As a result, this reduces the explanatory power of Johnson and Scott's research into the effect of anxiety on EWT.

The view that weapon focus is an explanation for the inaccuracy of memory recall has been challenged by research evidence. Valentine et al. (2003) investigated real-life crimes and the presence of a weapon by analysing data from a questionnaire completed by 640 real eyewitnesses who attempted to identify the suspects in 314 line-ups organised by the Metropolitan Police in London.

They found that the presence of a weapon had no effect on the outcome of correctly identifying the suspect. The findings show that the presence of a weapon does not reduce recall accuracy.

As a result, this lowers the credibility of the weapon-focus effect as an explanation of why the accuracy of EWT may be poor.

Furthermore, the inverted-U explanation has been criticised because it is too simplistic as an explanation. Anxiety is difficult to define and measure because it has many elements – cognitive, behavioural, emotional and physical. The inverted-U explanation assumes that one of these is linked to poor performance – physiological (physical) arousal. The explanation fails to account for other factors, for example, the effect of the emotional experience of witnessing a crime (e.g. terror, fear) on the accuracy of memory.

Finally, Yuille and Cutshall's research has also been criticised for having low internal validity. This is because they had little control over any extraneous variables that may have occurred. For example, they would not have had control during the five-month period after the crime had happened.

Variables such as witnesses' post-event discussions (e.g. co-witnesses, shop owner) or questions asked by the police may have had an impact on the accurate recall of what happened. This is a problem for the study because, if witnesses had conferred, they might have induced false memories and believed they saw something which may not have happened. As a result, this lowers the credibility of Yuille and Cutshall's research into the effect of anxiety on the accuracy of EWT.

The cognitive interview (CI)

Identification questions

Q79 Below are five evaluative statements about the cognitive interview. Which two statements are correct?

Circle three letters only.

The cognitive interview...   **[3 marks]**

A. Can only be used in Western cultures.

B. Takes longer than the standard interview.

C. Involves unethical treatment of witnesses.

D. Requires special training of police officers.

E. Cannot be used to interview children.

Q80 Below are statements about the cognitive interview. Identify the correct statements.

Circle one letter only.

Which component does not belong to the cognitive interview technique?   **[1 mark]**

A. Context reinstatement

B. Method of loci

C. Changed perspective

D. Report everything

E. Recall in reverse order

Q81 Below are statements about the cognitive interview. Identify the correct statements.

Circle one letter only.

The witness is asked to recall the events in a backward order. This is called: **[1 mark]**

A. Context reinstatement

B. Method of loci

C. Changed perspective

D. Report everything

E. Recall in reverse order

Q82 Below are statements about the cognitive interview. Identify the correct statements.

Circle one letter only.

The witness is told not to withhold any information when recalling. This is called: **[1 mark]**

    A. Context reinstatement

    B. Method of loci

    C. Changed perspective

    D. Report everything

    E. Recall in reverse order

Short-response questions

Q83 Explain what is meant by the term 'cognitive interview'. **[3 marks]**

The cognitive interview is a technique used by the police to help them retrieve more accurate memories when interviewing eyewitnesses. There are four components to the technique that use different retrieval cue strategies to help memory recall. The components are context reinstatement, report everything, recall in reverse order, and changed perspective.

Q84 Explain the 'context reinstatement' technique used in the cognitive interview and how this might improve the accuracy of memory recall. **[4 marks]**

The witness trying to mentally recreate an image of the situation will retrieve more information, including details of the environment, such as the weather conditions, and the individual's emotional state, including their feelings at the time of the incident. The notion is based on the context-dependent forgetting theory. If the context and feelings of the individual are similar for recall to the original situation, these will act as cues and help trigger more information from memory recall.

Q85 Explain the 'report everything' technique used in the cognitive interview and how this might improve the accuracy of memory recall. **[4 marks]**

The witness is encouraged not to hold back any information but to report everything they can remember about the incident regardless of how unimportant the information may seem to them. Reporting trivial matters is important as it may help trigger more information from memory. This is because memories are interconnected with one another, so that recollection of one item may then trigger a whole lot of other memories.

Q86 Explain the 'report everything' technique used in the cognitive interview and how this might improve the accuracy of memory recall. **[4 marks]**

The witness is asked to describe the scene in a different chronological order, in other words, to work backwards in time through the events they witnessed, from the end to the beginning. This is done to prevent people from reporting their 'expectations' of how the events must have happened rather than what happened. It also prevents dishonesty, as it is harder for people to produce an untruthful account if they have to reverse it.

Q87 Explain the 'changed perspective' technique used in the cognitive interview and how this might improve the accuracy of memory recall. **[4 marks]**

The witness is asked to try to imagine how the incident would have appeared from the viewpoint of one of the other witnesses. Using a changed perspective is believed to help increase the accuracy of recall because it reduces/disrupts the eyewitness's use of prior knowledge, expectations and schemas when asked to recall. For example, the schema you have for a particular setting (e.g. going into a shop) generates expectations of what would have happened, so the pre-existing schema is recalled rather than what actually happened.

Q88 Explain how a cognitive interview differs from a standard interview. **[4 marks]**

A standard interview has an unstructured question format, which often involves the interviewer asking a lot of questions ('what?', 'where?', 'how?'), that may require a forced choice answer e.g. What colour was the getaway car? This increases the possibility of misleading questions resulting in recall error. The cognitive interview follows a structured format with four elements that include context reinstatement (CR), reporting everything (RE), recall from a changed perspective (CP), and recall in reverse order (RO). These techniques use different retrieval cues to increase memory recall and reduce misleading questions from the interviewer to reduce recall error.

Q89 Describe one research study related to the cognitive interview. **[4 marks]**

Geiselman et al. (1986) carried out a laboratory experiment by comparing the effectiveness of the original cognitive interview (CI) with a standard police interview. Participants initially viewed a simulated violent crime film, and 48 hours later, they were interviewed, face-to-face, by police officers using a CI or standard interview (SI). They found that the cognitive interview produced an average of 17% more accurate information recall than the standard police interview. The findings show that under laboratory conditions, the CI is more effective than the SI for enhancing both the amount of information and the accuracy of eyewitness recall.

Application questions

 When Mario was walking home from work, he noticed a white car on the opposite side of the road. The car suddenly stopped next to a woman walking along the pavement. Then, three men jumped out of the car and dragged the woman inside the car. The abductors drove off with the victim in the car. All Mario can remember was the woman screaming: "Help me, help me!"

The police questioned Mario using the cognitive interview technique. Explain how the police could use the cognitive interview to investigate what Mario could remember. In your answer, you must refer to details from the passage above. **[4 marks]**

The police may ask Mario to 'report everything' he saw. This means Mario is encouraged not to hold back any information about the incident regardless of how unimportant it may seem. For example, Mario may have remembered the van behind the white car that had passed the red traffic lights. This may be relevant as the occupants of the van could also have been part of the kidnapper's gang.

The police will then ask Mario to recall the events in reverse order. This time, Mario is asked to work backwards in time through the events he witnessed. Research evidence suggests that by changing the sequence of recall, witnesses can look at each stage of the event separately and this helps extract more details of the event when compared to a forward-order recall. For example, the very last thing Mario may remember is the back of the white car, where he saw a sticker of a country's flag next to the number plate.

Long-response questions

 Q91 Describe and evaluate the cognitive interview as a method of improving the accuracy of memory.

[16 marks]

Geiselman et al. (1984) developed the cognitive interview (CI) technique to help the police in the process of interviewing by reducing recall errors and to extract more information from the witness than a standard interview (SI). The technique uses four different retrieval-cue strategies to help increase memory recall and reduce recall error. The first component of the technique is the 'context reinstatement', which requires the witnesses to mentally recreate an image of the situation (e.g. environment, such as the weather conditions) and the individual's emotional state (feelings) at the time of the incident. The second technique is 'report everything'. Witnesses are encouraged not to hold back any information regardless of how unimportant some of it may seem to them. Reporting trivial matters is important as it may help trigger more information from memory. The next part is to recall in 'reverse order'.

The witness is asked to work backwards in time through the events they witnessed. This is done to prevent people from reporting their 'expectations' of how the events must have happened rather than what happened. Finally, the witness is asked to try to imagine how the incident would have appeared from the viewpoint of one of the other main witnesses at the event or scene, which is known as 'changed perspective'. Changed perspective is believed to help increase the accuracy of recall because it reduces the eyewitness use of prior knowledge and expectations when asked to recall.

There is supporting research evidence for the cognitive interview technique. Geiselman et al. (1986) carried out a laboratory experiment by comparing the effectiveness of the original CI with a standard police interview. Participants initially viewed a simulated violent crime film, and 48 hours later, they were interviewed, face-to-face, by police officers using a CI or standard interview (SI) technique. They found that the cognitive interview produced an average of 17% more accurate information recall than the standard police interview. The findings suggest that under laboratory conditions, the CI is more effective than the SI for enhancing both the amount of information and the accuracy of eyewitness recall.

There are several problems with the cognitive interview technique. The CI procedure is designed to enhance the quantity of accurate recall without compromising the quality of that information. However, it may be that effectiveness has largely been in terms of quantity. Kohnken et al. (1999) carried out a meta-analysis of over 53 studies that found an average 33% increase in correct recall using CI compared with a standard police interview. However, there was also an increase in recall error, with 17% incorrect details reported with CI than with SI. Therefore, it is important that police officers need to take this into account when evaluating witness accounts as the CI may not guarantee accuracy.

Furthermore, the CI procedure does not help with face recognition and person identification. For example, Newlands et al. (1999) found that the descriptions of criminals using the cognitive interview technique were no better than descriptions resulting from a standard interview. Also, CI was not very effective with children under the age of six years. Small children have difficulty in understanding the requirements of the CI procedure. For example, young children had difficulty with the 'change perspective' instruction. This suggests that CI is only effective to use at a certain age, notably, with older children and adults.

A final limitation of the CI is that it is time-consuming. Police are reluctant to use CI because it takes much more time than the standard police interview. More time is needed to establish rapport with the witness to allow them to relax. Kebbell and Wagstaff (1997) point out that the CI also requires special training, and many forces have not been able to provide more than a few hours. This means it is unlikely that the 'proper' version of the CI is used. This may explain why police have not been that impressed by this technique, and the use of the CI has not been widespread.

Answers to identification questions

The multi-store model of memory

Q1 A = Sensory memory (or sensory register)

   B = Short-term memory (STM)

   C = Long-term memory (LTM)

   D = Rehearsal loop

Q2 Sensory register = unlimited

   STM (Duration) = 18-30 sec

   STM (Coding) = Acoustic

   LTM (Coding) = Semantic

Q3

	Short-term memory	Long-term memory
Encoding		C
Capacity	A	
Duration	B	

Working memory model

Q23 Boxes B, C, D

Types of long-term memory

Q37 A

Q38 A

Q39 B

Explanations for forgetting: Interference

Q50 B

Q51 A

Explanations for forgetting: Retrieval failure

Q57 B

EWT: misleading information

Q64 A and D

The cognitive interview

Q79 B, D and E

Q80 B

Q81 E

Q82 D